ROLE-PLAYING GAMES

BY KIZZI ROBERTS

Apex is distributed by North Star Editions:
sales@northstareditions.com | 888-417-0195

Produced for Apex by Red Line Editorial.

Photographs ©: Shutterstock Images, cover, 1, 4–5, 6–7, 8, 9, 10–11, 12–13, 14–15, 18, 20–21, 22–23, 24, 26, 27, 29; Christian Bertrand/Alamy, 16–17

Library of Congress Control Number: 2022920696

ISBN
978-1-63738-575-3 (hardcover)
978-1-63738-629-3 (paperback)
978-1-63738-731-3 (ebook pdf)
978-1-63738-683-5 (hosted ebook)

Printed in the United States of America
Mankato, MN
082023

NOTE TO PARENTS AND EDUCATORS

Apex books are designed to build literacy skills in striving readers. Exciting, high-interest content attracts and holds readers' attention. The text is carefully leveled to allow students to achieve success quickly. Additional features, such as bolded glossary words for difficult terms, help build comprehension.

TABLE OF CONTENTS

CHAPTER 1

ON A QUEST

A girl plays role-playing games (RPGs) on her computer. In one game, she is a wizard. She finds magical items. In another, she is a troll. She explores a cave.

In RPGs, players often explore mysterious places such as castles or caves.

In *Kingdom Hearts*, players visit and try to save many worlds.

The girl plays some RPGs alone. She completes **quests**. Some quests are short. Others take hours to finish.

SAVING GAMES

Most modern RPGs let players stop and save at any time. In older games, players had to reach save points. Some of these points were at the ends of levels. Others were places on the map.

Many RPG characters are hunters or fighters.

For other games, the girl plays online with friends. They work together as a team. Each friend plays a different role.

Online games let people play with or against gamers from around the world.

CHAPTER 2

WHAT IS AN RPG?

RPGs are games where players take part in stories as **fictional** characters. Players fight battles or solve problems. Their actions shape how the story unfolds.

RPG characters may fight dragons or other monsters.

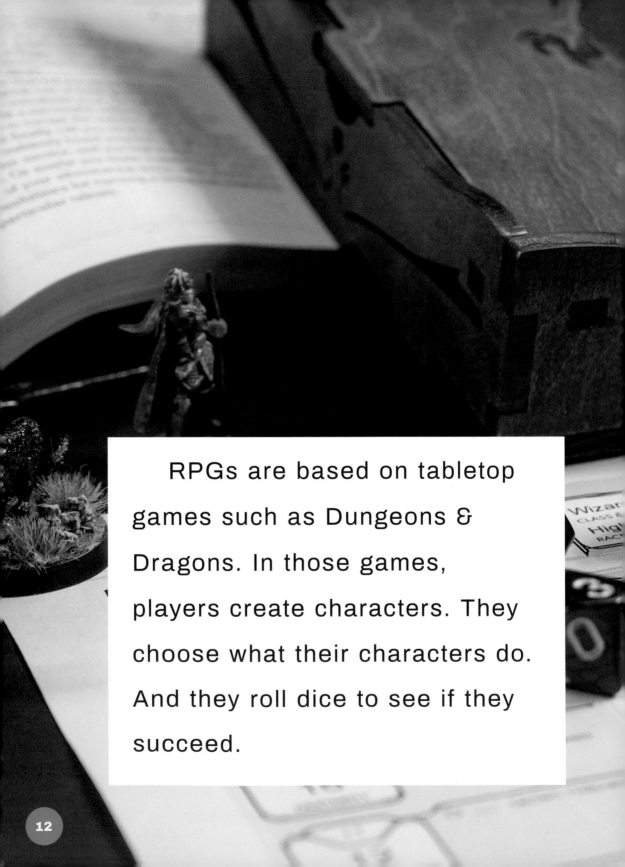

RPGs are based on tabletop games such as Dungeons & Dragons. In those games, players create characters. They choose what their characters do. And they roll dice to see if they succeed.

Dungeons & Dragons first came out in 1974. People still play it today.

By the 1980s, many people used gaming systems to play RPGs at home.

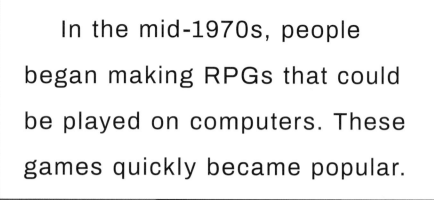

In the mid-1970s, people began making RPGs that could be played on computers. These games quickly became popular.

EARLY RPGS

The first RPG video games had very simple **graphics**. Their stories were simple, too. Players mainly fought monsters. Over time, games gave players more choices and more ways to explore.

CHAPTER 3

TYPES OF RPGS

Today, there are many different types of RPGs. Action games focus on fighting. Strategy games focus on skill and planning.

Final Fantasy XV is an action RPG. Players try to save a kingdom.

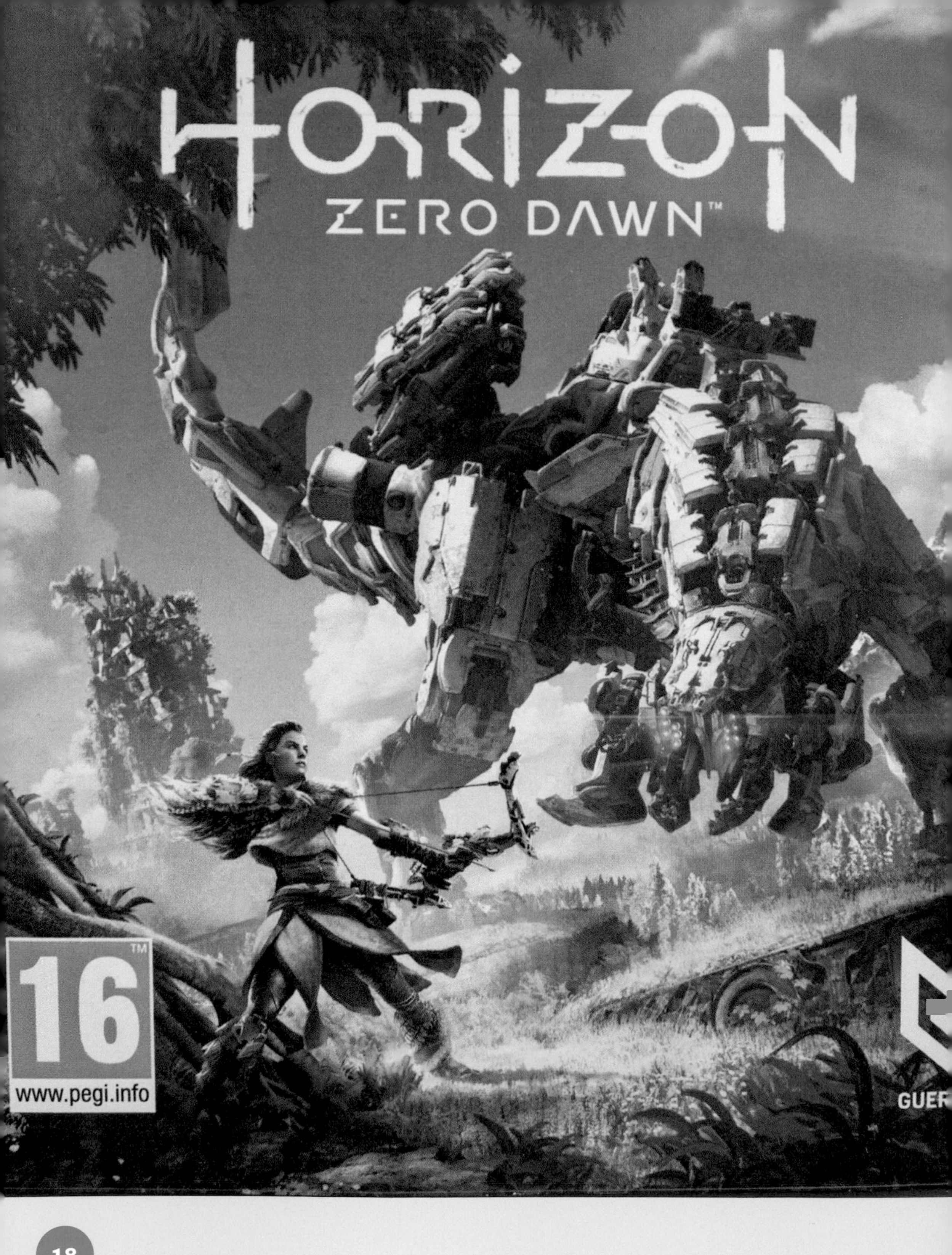
HORIZON
ZERO DAWN™
16
www.pegi.info

Other games focus on exploration. These games often have large maps. Players travel and explore. They also complete quests.

OPEN WORLD

Some RPGs have open-world maps. In these games, players choose what to do and where to go. They can also complete quests in any order.

Horizon: Zero Dawn is an open-world game. Players hunt and explore.

Winning fights is a common way to build experience in RPGs.

In all RPGs, players work to improve their characters. They gain skills and **experience**. They also collect money. Then they can get better weapons or supplies.

FAST FACT

Some RPGs take more than 200 hours to finish.

CHAPTER 4

WAYS TO PLAY

People can play RPGs on **consoles** or computers. Some RPGs are designed for smartphones, too.

Dragon Quest Walk is an RPG for smartphones. To play, gamers walk around in the real world.

For multiplayer games, a few friends may share the same console. Other players join massively multiplayer online role-playing games (MMORPGs). These games can have thousands of players.

FAST FACT

World of Warcraft is a popular MMORPG. In 2022, more than 1 million people played each day.

In MMORPGs, many players all join the same online world.

People travel from around the world to attend Gamescom. This convention is in Cologne, Germany.

Some gamers compete in **tournaments**. They may also go to **conventions**. At these events, people can play and learn about games. They often dress up as their favorite characters.

GAMESCOM

Gaming conventions bring RPG fans together. Gamescom is one of the biggest. It takes place in Germany each year. In 2022, more than 265,000 people attended. They came from many countries.

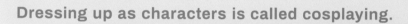
Dressing up as characters is called cosplaying.

COMPREHENSION QUESTIONS

Write your answers on a separate piece of paper.

1. Write a few sentences describing what all RPGs have in common.

2. Would you rather join a multiplayer game or play on your own? Why?

3. In which type of RPG do players focus on fighting?

   A. action
   B. strategy
   C. open world

4. How are RPGs and tabletop games alike?

   A. Both are based on real-life events.
   B. Both let players choose what to do.
   C. Both tell players exactly what to do.

5. What does **divided** mean in this book?

RPG characters are often divided into groups called classes. Each class has different abilities.

    A. cut in half
    B. sorted by type
    C. gotten rid of

6. What does **designed** mean in this book?

People can play RPGs on computers or consoles. Some RPGs are designed for smartphones, too.

    A. made to be used on a certain device
    B. made to be played by rolling dice
    C. made to be taken apart into many pieces

Answer key on page 32.

GLOSSARY

abilities
Things someone can do.

consoles
Devices that people use to play video games at home.

conventions
Big gatherings where people go to learn or buy things.

experience
Skills or knowledge as a result of doing something.

fantasy
Stories that involve magic, often set in made-up worlds.

fictional
Made up as part of a story.

graphics
The images players see during a game.

quests
Long or hard journeys to find objects or complete tasks.

tournaments
Competitions where players try to win several games or rounds.

TO LEARN MORE

BOOKS

Abdo, Kenny. *Naruto: Ninja and Hero*. Minneapolis: Abdo
  Publishing, 2022.

Rathburn, Betsy. *Online Gaming*. Minneapolis: Bellwether
  Media, 2021.

Troupe, Thomas Kingsley. *Fantastic Worlds: The Inspiring
  Truth Behind Popular Role-Playing Video Games*. North
  Mankato, MN: Capstone Press, 2019.

ONLINE RESOURCES

Visit **www.apexeditions.com** to find links and resources
related to this title.

ABOUT THE AUTHOR

Kizzi Roberts lives with her family in southern Missouri. She
has traveled with a circus, competed in Brazilian jiu-jitsu,
and gone scuba diving in Thailand. She also enjoys writing,
reading, and playing video games.

INDEX

ANSWER KEY:
1. Answers will vary; 2. Answers will vary; 3. A; 4. B; 5. B; 6. A